# Rebuilt from the Ashes

Gina Ruiz

You floated through life in a cocoon of innocence

You knew true happiness and had no fears

Until a storm approached

And shattered your shell

Now you're free

And swimming in a bitter sea of tears.

You're well versed with the cliché of yelling

At the main character in a horror movie.

It is so obvious to you where the danger lies.

So how can you go through your life so deaf

While everyone around you yells warnings?

How can you so blindly follow

When everyone else sees him

For the monster he is?

Your world was grey until he appeared

He brought with him a magnificent array of colors

You experienced a warmth and beauty

You never knew.

He left as quick as he came,

Trailing his rainbow behind him.

Now you're left with grey

And memories of beautiful hues.

You're so blinded by the colors

That were once so bright

That now you can't even see

The paintbrush is in your own hands.

Sometimes in the dark

When everything is quiet

There is a calm

That washes over me.

In these moments I look back

On when I almost left

This place that I call home

And I wonder If that journey would have been

The future always holds promises

The past is full of regrets

The present is full of emptiness and things we'd like to forget.

So hungry for your love,

So desperate for your approval

When you whispered 'I love you'

I never noticed you weren't looking at me.

Depression is dependable.

When no one else notices or seems to care,

Depression is always there.

Why can't I look in the mirror

And treat the image on the other side

The way I know she needs?

Why do I view her as the villain

When I know all she has endured?

Why can't I look her in the eye

And tell her it will be okay?

When you bleed, people stop to ask how.

When you cry, people stop to ask why.

But when you smile, nobody stops.

Because it isn't worth their while.

You constantly rip apart

Any chance you have at happiness

So crippled by self-doubt

But starving for affection.

Instead of making changes

And getting what you need,

You cry and lie and twist the truth To
destroy those who are what you

will

**never**

be.

Is there ever an end to feeling

Like you'll never be enough?

Why can't you love me for who I am

Instead of what you want me to be?

Sometimes people come into our lives

Just to shake things up.

They change what we thought we knew,

For better or worse.

They become what we find comfortable

And just as we settle in to our new normal

They leave us in the night to pick up the pieces

And blindly try to fit them together again.

But now our puzzle has changed

And nothing seems to fit.

And then you're left

To either work through the challenge

*And keep going*

Or to become stagnant

And always looking back at things

You'll never be able to touch again.

I sit in silence with my thoughts.

You always asked me to be open with you

But I wonder how you would react

If I cut my heart open and let It

All

Pour

Out

You're like a song that is stuck in my head.

I can't seem to escape you,

No matter how hard I try.

Even when I listen to other songs

And beg for them to stay instead,

You're always there.

You used to be so full of adventure.

You were ready for anything.

But then you got knocked down again

And now you can't seem to recover.

You hide from your missed opportunities

And cling to your glory days.

All you need to do is get up.

But you're stuck on the slippery slope of regret.

Sometimes when I walk

Through the house at night,

I still see you.

And for a moment, everything feels right.

Like it used to.

But then I remember that you're gone.

It kills me less and less each time.

And I think that hurts *more*.

I only exist to you when you're lonely.

My only worth to you is my body.

I am a toy you can forget on the shelf,

Only remembering me When you're bored.

I make art to show the world how I feel.

Maybe that's why I destroy it as soon as I finish.

Being vulnerable

Has never looked good on me anyway.

You told me I was the only one you loved

As you kissed me goodbye

And sent me on my way

Back into the mass of girls

You so effortlessly established.

Just hoping to hear you say it one more time.

I like the way the sun feels on my skin.

It fills me with a warmth that works its way down

Through my bones.

Down to the innermost depths of my soul

Allowing me a respite

From the numbing cold inside of me.

Even if only until the next cloud passes by.

You want so badly to be enough

That you threw away your entire life

Just for the possibility that this time

You might make it.

The silver lining

Of having everyone doubt you

Is how easy it is to surprise them.

The view out of my window

Is like a snow globe.

Beautiful, pristine and quiet.

And for a moment,

I can pretend that nothing is wrong.

Be your own hero

The others are all frauds anyway.

It is an interesting phenomenon how easily

Your feelings for a person can change.

One comment

One gesture

And suddenly your opinion has shifted.

I often wonder how many people

I've caused to change their opinion of me.

I can only hope it was for the better.

But based on how many people have left,

I assume it was for the worse.

When I put myself last,

Bending over backwards for everyone,

I was always surrounded by people.

I felt loved.

The day I started to put myself first,

I was suddenly alone.

Everyone says to value yourself

But what they really mean

Is to value yourself after them.

We often get so preoccupied with thinking

About what could have been

That we can't see what could be.

Constantly looking back

Will only lead to a crash.

Don't forget to look at where you're going.

Slow decay is worse than a quick destruction.

It is much easier to grieve

And move on from a sudden loss.

Watching it happen and being in denial

Is torture.

Can you ever fully recover

Knowing you could have saved it?

I exist in an existential crisis.

Too afraid to live, too afraid to die.

I remember the smell of the summer air.

The sounds of crickets filled the night.

I wish I could go back to our time together.

Not yet realizing that nothing stays.

You left without a word

As if we were both aware this was over.

How was I supposed to know

That kiss was our last?

You never told me this was your way

Of saying goodbye.

They say in seven years,

The skin regenerates enough that its new.

That means it takes seven years

Before I have skin

That you have never touched.

So why do I *still* feel you?

I lived in the dark for so long

That when you came around

And brought your light

I was afraid to let you in.

You showed me that its okay

To face things in the light.

I showed you the dark

Doesn't have to be a scary place.

We were always in a rush to grow up.

But now that we're here,

We're longing for the past.

We were so focused on getting out

That we never learned to love where we are.

What if the princess saves herself this time?

What if she slays her own dragon?

What if she rides off

Into the sunset on her own?

What if she doesn't need a prince

To make it all okay?

She tells me I'm beautiful, says she loves me.

I tell her I love her but they're hollow words.

My emotions are empty.

I disappeared silently to let her free.

I never felt guilty.

Even knowing she must have hurt.

I watched you walk up to me,

Caress my face with your hand.

I looked deep into your eyes

As you wrapped your hand around my throat.

I heard you tell me I deserved this.

I heard you say you loved me

That this was all my fault.

I took it all in

Before everything faded to black.

Driving at night,

We always stopped at the beach.

The silence broken

Only by the waves coming in.

We buried our feet in the sand

And for a moment

I forgot I was broken inside.

Walking back to the car,

It would all hit me again.

As cold as the night air on my bare skin.

Fearless in our youth,

We took risks without realizing.

Looking back, we wonder how we survived.

In our current lives, we're distant.

Our fear and anxiety

Driving us away from the world.

From each other.

I want to paint a picture

Of the greatest wonder I've ever seen.

But for all the money in the world,

The only thing

I would be able to come up with

Is <u>you</u>.

I think of you when my socks don't match.

I think of you when it rains.

I think of you every minute.

I can't get you out of my brain.

I want you to see that I'm doing well.

I want you to care.

I want you to remember **I'm alive**.

The world stopped spinning

The moment he walked in.

I wanted him and he wanted to know me.

I had too many walls

And he could never be strong enough

To break through.

Instead of letting him try,

I faked disinterest and let it die.

I thought I knew who I was.

Then I met you.

Now I don't know which way is up

And I wouldn't change it for the world.

We are often told how our lives should go.

What we should do and when.

Don't be afraid to stand on a table

With your fist in the air

And declare war against the standards.

Never be afraid to live wildly

Or to love fiercely.

Be ravenous for knowledge.

And never live with regret.

I set fire to the bridge you left behind.

Desperately trying

To rebuild it from the ashes.

My body is an empty canvas

And with every new color or piece of metal

I am reminded that even though

I have been broken and battered

I am still beautiful.

How many showers do I have to take

How many gallons of water do I have to drink

To finally be able to wash you away

I've never been good at math.

But I've always been good at telling

When something doesn't add up.

I knew it was over

Before you even kissed her.

I rebuilt myself from the ashes.

Engulfed in the flames,

I was forged stronger than before.

Like a phoenix, I am reborn.

**You will never break me.**

I drove past your old house the other day.

There's new paint and it looks so different.

I hope you're as happy now

As we used to be then.

I loved you with my heart

Before my brain realized it.

I would do anything to protect you

From the danger and harm of life

But sometimes you need to dive in headfirst.

And I can't be the one to pull you in.

You were my rock when I needed you.

But you slowly moved farther away.

Our relationship became one sided.

I left your wedding broken.

I would hate you if I cared about you.

All you can do

Is tear everyone down around you.

You're your own worst enemy

How long will you throw the blame

On everyone else?

You can't always play the victim.

Do you wake up every day

And know the sun came out for you?

Are you aware the rain is falling for you?

Do you look in the mirror

And realize you are worth

More than you see?

Happy birthday you said

With one hand

You gave me a half used lighter

With the other

You waved goodbye.

As the tide rolls in

And everything is engulfed in water

Embrace the change

And remember things will be okay.

I looked through the window

At the life we were supposed to share.

You looked happy with her.

I threw a rock through the window.

I always felt so out of place

So desperate to get as far away as possible

Seeking a place I could feel at home.

Now that I have you,

It doesn't matter where I go.

I'll always have a place I call home with you.

I miss laying next to you.

Feeling your warmth and knowing

That no matter what,

You'd be here waiting for me.

The world is a big place.

It's a miracle the stars aligned

In just the right way to bring us together.

Even if it was only for a moment.

It wasn't until I was alone

That I truly started living.

When you're on your own,

You become a priority.

You are the piece my soul was missing.

Why was it so hard for you to stay

And be happy

But so easy for you to leave

And never look back

As the water from the shower

Rolls down my back

I imagine it taking all my worries

And washing them down the drain.

But I know there will never be enough water

To rid me of them all.

We hide our emotions

Behind thinly veiled jokes

And awkward silences.

Too afraid to say what we mean

Until the other has already left.

You gave your heart to someone

Who was already looking for the next one

Before you even finished saying your name.

As the years go by it gets easier to see

That many of the people you looked up to

Are just as much of a mess as you are.

We were supposed to go out

In a blaze of glory

Instead we fizzled out and were forgotten

Like an old match burnt to the end

And discarded on the floor.

Why did it take me so long to realize

That I am the only one with the ability

To write my story

They say hindsight is 20/20

And ignorance is bliss.

That's why I know I'm better off without you

And I don't want to know what I missed.

Every time you lash out unprovoked

And claim we mean nothing

You prove over and over

That you wish we cared.

Self-sabotage can be so subtle

That I often don't realize what I've done

Until I pull the knife away and realize

It was in my own back.

I act like a sponge and soak up

All the anxieties and problems

Of those around me.

Creating problems and scenarios for myself

That don't exist in my life.

And yet I lay awake at night

With my head filled

With imaginary issues and no solutions.

We project what we want people to see

All the bad and mediocre

Building up around us

Unaware that we're all frauds

Just forcing an image

Of who we wish we could be

Going back to where I used to live

Catching up with those I've left behind

Often feels like I've landed on another planet

Somehow familiar but entirely new

Stuck feeling like I no longer belong.

A star needs darkness to shine

But how much is enough

Before the star starts to shine

Through all the darkness that surrounds it

I am only truly myself when I am alone.

The me that everyone thinks they know

Is a fraud

A version of myself

That can hide the weird and ugly

Everyone sees a different version

As I struggle to keep up

And long for the moment I can be myself

I'm at my best at 2am

When the rest of the world is asleep

And it feels like I'm the only one on the planet

There are no worries, no fears

Just me and the silence

Loving you was like agreeing

To the terms and conditions

Without really reading

I was blindsided by your expectations

And your lack of sincerity

While you demanded everything I was

Follow your heart

But don't forget to bring your head.

I spent ten years trying to rid my life of you

It felt so good to finally be honest

When you said you hated yourself

I said I did too

I always thought love was big gestures

Movie worthy moments

It was never love

You were just playing your part

It's summer again

You're not here

And I've never felt better

Hold my hand as we jump into the deep end

The weights on our ankles tied tight

You know how to swim, right?

You always hated my individuality

It meant I didn't listen to your every word

I wasn't your perfect little doll

I pretended to love you

And I think that was worse

Than being honest in the first place

And breaking your heart

I gave you everything I had

You couldn't even give me a goodbye

The lights went out

Long before they should have

Just a flicker and then back again

I took it as my sign

To pack my bag and move on

One day I hope to love myself

As much as I loved you

At least I know it will be reciprocated this time

I spend my time running

From the demons I created

Because facing them means facing you

Thank you to everyone who pushed me to face my fears and share my creation.

Made in the USA
Lexington, KY
18 February 2019